From Dusk to Dawn

Or Remembering How to Live Again

By B. R. Underhill

From Dusk to Dawn;
Or Remembering How to Live Again

Copyright © 2019 Benjamin Underhill

From Dusk to Dawn;
Or Remembering How to Live Again

FIRST EDITION, Paperback
ISBN 978-0-578-52625-6

10 9 8 7 6 5 4 3 2 1

Illustrations Copyright © 2019 Rhea Rifflard,

Book and Cover Design by Benjamin Underhill
Published through Kindle Direct Publishing
Email questions to BenUnderhillBooks@gmail.com

All characters appearing in this work are fictitious. Any resemblance to real persons, living or dead, is completely coincidental.

While the author has made every effort to provide accurate telephone numbers, Internet addresses, and other contact information at the time of publication, neither the publisher nor the author assumes any responsibility for errors or for changes that occur after publication.

FROM DUSK
TO DAWN

or remembering
how to live again

Dedicated to You
For Never Giving Up
No Matter How Difficult it Got.

"Believe in your dreams.
They were given to you
for a reason."

-Katrina Mayer

"8:15 pm"

Too many times your brain will overload,
And you'll find yourself there again in limbo.
You'll sit there,
Numb to reality,
Gazing out like a ghost.

That pressure in your gut will weigh in,
Saying, "This might actually be it."

"You might actually go through with it this time."

It will all simply stop.
Everything around you will drift on
And on,
And on,
While you
Just
Float.

You'll feel stuck at first,
Finding no escape from this new reality.
You'll think yourself a skeleton
As you search desperately for the light
At the end of the tunnel,
Only to reach your hand up
Toward a single twinkling star.
It will capture your attention.
You'll experience your every being
Telling you to go.

You will take the first step
And realize how far you have to go.
Looking up, you'll finally understand
That you don't realize it's rock bottom
Until you finally hit it;
There's nowhere else to go but up.

Thus, begins your endless climb.

"8:19 pm"

I wrote my suicide letter
In the notepad app on my phone.
I outlined every detail
Decidedly derived through existential outliers;
Outliers that exist
On the misanthropist spectrum of loneliness.

Reverse the referendum of dreaming too high
Because I am the dreamer who will get lost
In his own nightmares.

I signed my note the best I could,
Dotting my "i" to finish up my life.
I loved the way it looked and cherished it,
All 79 words of it.

"8:22 pm"

My current emptiness
Is a specific method of falling deeper
Down the rabbit hole,
Meeting Alice in the psych ward.
It's a testament,
An investment,
Retraining my head
To maybe just work a little bit better
And to forget the unforgettable.

Too often it's too hard to get back,
Turning the keys over and over,
Hoping the engine will start again,
Fixing the stall.
I try getting back on my feet
And lie with a smile that everything is okay,
Even though nothing is,
Even though I'm a walking shell
Not even flinching at slit wrists
Or cleaning up the bloody mess
And simply moving forward.

Why is it no surprise
That crazy attracts crazy?

Suck it up buttercup,
And take another shot
And another hit
And another shot
And another hit
And another and another and another
Over
And over
And over again
Until I am numb.

At least when I'm numb I forget,
And forgetting helps for now.
When it hurts that bad,
It's better than falling
Down the rabbit hole again.

"8:31 pm"

I consistently destroy myself
Simply so I can feel something.

These shattering moments entrap me:
Alcohol
And drugs
And your lips.

Please bring me to rehab
So that I can deal with the withdrawals
And finally move on from you.

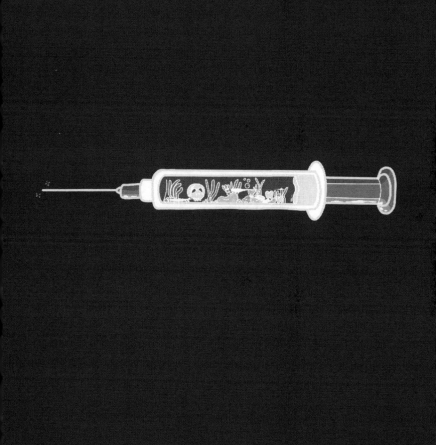

"8:35 pm"

I am circling above reality like a scavenger
Endlessly searching for a scrap of life.

I am desperate for a taste
Of anything
That will make it all seem worth it.

I am here,
I am surviving,
And my heart aches for it to be something,
Anything,
More than simply that.

"8:38 pm"

With each pen stroke,
I become more omniscient
Of my demise,
Of my reprise.

I turn away and hit replay,
Praying to find the mistake,
Yet inevitably repeating it:
Yet again, the quietus of me.

It's a side effect of my vices,
Drug induced feelings of normality
Are now normal,
And apparently
I'm the happiest I've ever been
While simultaneously being the most alone.

"8:42 pm"

I'm not sure what to say anymore.
I lost a lot of hope along the way,
And continuing to search for more
Has become as difficult as finding Atlantis.

I lost myself a long time ago,
And I'm still finding the pieces,
So, I'm sorry if I feel incomplete at times.
I'm trying.
Really, I'm trying my best.
And even that doesn't seem to be enough.

"8:44 pm"

You can tell the exact moment
A poet is at his lowest.

It is not in his sunken-in eyes or weak smile,
Nor is it the fact
That getting out of bed is impossible.
No, the sign is not there physically,
Not emotionally,
Not even mentally.
The sign is as abrupt as it is evident.

The poet is at his lowest
When even the words he so dearly loves
Cannot express what he feels.

And the writing suddenly stops.

"8:47 pm"

Believing in myself
Became one of the hardest things to do,
Second only
To keeping myself alive.

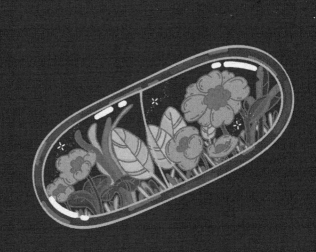

"8:55 pm"

Do my words even matter?
Do they have the same ego-cutting effect
As Bukowski or Hemmingway?
Will I ever sit among the greats?
Or will I merely aspire in their shadows
To create something,
Anything,
That might help you feel something?

"9:02 pm"

I want to experience the world
And the way that the world should be.
The way that I and the world are right now
Are not the way I want it to be;
In fact, its intricacy
Is my lack of sensibility.
It's my lack of sensitivity.
It's my lack of willing to be.
I simply want to explore my mind
And everything around me;
I want to explore my reality,
And yet I am lost in my own mind,
Holding myself back,
Even with a desire to be up among the stars.

I'm so obliviated by the world
And the way that the world is
And the way that the world is for me
Is not going that well.
But, alas, I do these things
Because I want to feel again.
I want to feel like my mind is creative,
I want to feel as if I am a creative,
As if I will be a genius yet again;
As if my life will have meaning yet again.
No wince, no wonder,
No wonder I feel no pain.
The intricacy of the poem that goes in and out,
Everything that is going
Between the lines is breathing through them
And finding time to stand still.
Perhaps the world will not be at peace again
Until I am dead,
Or until I am alive,
And I do not know which I need to be right now.
All I know
Is that I need to at least find something.

"9:09 pm"

I am cynical when it comes to love,
Yet it has not always been this way.
I know this,
Truly know this,
Because I still love you so fucking much.

My heart drops
With every alcoholic kiss I see;
His hands on your hips,
And my arm hidden from the world
For reasons you told me never to do again.

However, that was when I thought,
Well, you made me believe,
That I meant something to you.
And now
I just want you out of my mind.

Please, please give me back my heart.
I don't think I can feel anything
With it in your hands anymore.

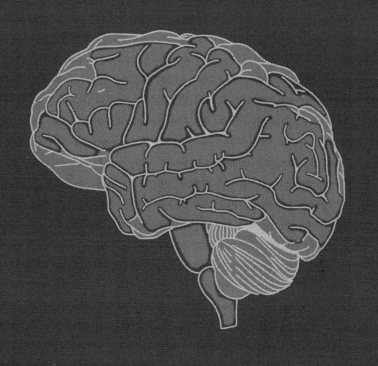

"9:12 pm"

This fear grabs hold of me,
Gripping my neck as I squirm for freedom.
I feel so lost as you sit there watching,
Eating popcorn as my life crumbles
As if it's a movie.

Clarity is my heroin
And I'm itching for my next fix.

Maybe I'll make sense of it all next time,
Or maybe next,
Or maybe next,
Or maybe I'll never get it,
And I'll end up broken;

Will you glue me back together?
Or will I remain shattered,
Subject to the elements?

"9:18 pm"

You don't really understand
What I'm actually dealing with.
I'm at DEFCON 1,
And my finger is on the big red button.
This type of nothing-left-to-lose is a gamble,
And all my chips are on my life.
I feel so lost and distorted in reality
That I find sanctuary
Only in my mind.
To be honest,
Even there doesn't feel safe anymore.
I get lost in my loneliness
Even though I'm rarely alone.
When I feed those thoughts though,
The further down the rabbit hole I go.

"9:21 pm"

I write and reminisce
About the darkness fairly often.
It's hard not to.
That era consumed my life twice now,
And all I can do
Is find a rope to pull myself up further.
Find the next foothold.
Take hold of the next rung.

It leaves me lost.
I struggle because I don't know what to do
Because I didn't plan this far ahead;
I thought I'd be dead by now.

So please,
If it takes me a moment to move on,
Know that I'm doing my best,
And sometimes,
That's all I can do.

"9:28 pm"

My mind is caged,
And I have the key,
Yet I serve time anyway.
I keep myself locked away,
Unable to allow my conscious to run free
Due to the fear of what may happen next.

I have the key in the keyhole.
Now all I need is the courage to turn it.

"9:33 pm"

I'm not sure if you know,
But I still love you.

And it's tearing me apart.

"9:39 pm"

Why are we still so connected?
We hate each other
Every damn moment
Except when we are in bed
With our bodies pressed together.

Why do you keep destroying me?
I have given everything,
Done nothing but love.
Now it's nothing but hate.

You bitch.

"9:45 pm"

I am a serial killer,
And yet the number of deaths are not recorded
In the obituaries in the newspapers
Nor the funerals at the parlor.
Instead, they are recorded
In the souls of the people
Whose lives I have touched,
Of the relationships I've found and lost
And wish to find again.

I am a serial killer in the sense
That when I leave
A little piece of me dies as I go.

My only victim
Has been myself.

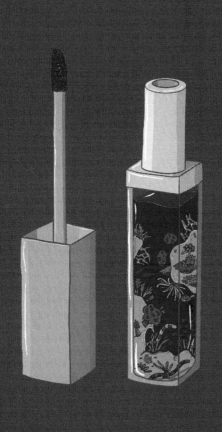

"9:55 pm"

I can see it in your eyes:
That hurt never goes away,
Does it?

It lurks,
Waiting for a moment of fallibility to strike.
It sits, festers, and rots away your true self,
And yet you still hold it in.

Please, take my hand,
Come with me toward hope.
Please don't let me lose you too.

"10:01 pm"

I am a melancholy optimist,
A feeler of unfelt dreams,
A remorseful man
Who prays and begs for you back.

I still imagine your unrequited love
Tearing into the fabric of my being.

Begging,
Begging,
I plead with you
To set me free
From the constraints of my reality.
Shall I go on?
I must,
For it is my truth
In my mind and in my soul.

Explode
And implode
Emotions
We rarely feel,
Or we feel nothing,
As I do and don't
In the latest hours
I manage to stay awake at night.

Where is my freedom?
Where is my peace?
Where is my hope?

I search tirelessly
In hopes of the answer
You refuse to tell me.

Damn you to hell,
Even if you were once my heaven.

"10:09 pm"

I always imagined summer
To be beaches and music festivals,
Not sunburns and losing you.

"10:13 pm"

It seems like my life
Has turned into repetition.

I write poem after poem about my exes,
And I don't even love them;
Or at least, I say I don't.

Their departure from my life
Leaves me wondering
Why they are still my muse,
Until I look back and see
That the poems fill the emptiness I feel.

"10:17 pm"

Dear You,

I'm sorry that things didn't work out. I'm sorry that I left you broken-hearted and numb, a feeling I know all too well. You deserve better. And I need to do better.

The unfortunate fact is we were victims of bad timing, and, well, I'm not sure if the timing will ever be right again.

To tell you the truth, I miss you. I miss your laughter and tears and every waking moment and sleepy kiss goodnight. I miss the way you would nuzzle into me, and I would hold you tight to let you know everything would be okay; I miss the way you would do the same for me.

I'm not sure if our paths will cross again. I wish I could've given you more, but I was tapped out, and I'm sorry for that too. If there's anything that comes out of it, I simply hope that you're happy.

Please. Please, chase your dreams and let your happiness come.

I'm sorry I could not be there for it.

Love Always,
Me

"10:22 pm"

And just like that,
The one I thought would stay forever
Was gone.

"10:29 pm"

When you left,
You turned off the "no"
Next to the "vacancy" sign in my heart,
Even though I wanted it on
Forever.

"10:31 pm"

I try to replace the taste of you
More and more each day
With the taste of alcohol and burning cigarettes;
The only problem is
Neither leave me craving more
Than the way I was addicted to you.

"10:34 pm"

I arrive here alone lately,
Tasting our favorite drink
And briefly dreaming of your lips.

My biggest mistake
Was thinking I'd move on.

"10:44 pm"

Perhaps my days are not numbered.
It is possible,
For I have no concept of reality.
Reality, I say. Not truth.
The truth cannot be reality
Because nothing so painful can be real.
Maybe this is why
You no longer exist in my mind.

"10:51 pm"

It's strange to think that mere months
Felt like years.
My introspective thought
Tells me to stop feeling again
While also feeling like I can feel.
The void expanded and consumed me,
Destroying my hope
Until I become too intoxicated
To remember.

Now, the void has collapsed.

"11:00 pm"

I believe my life is on pause,
Wishing to filter the insignificant.
Hopefully it will continue soon
And reach a point where maybe
"I'm fine" is sincere
And where neither of us want to die anymore.

"11:05 pm"

I felt something today.

I woke up,
Exhausted per usual,
Dreading every aching moment of the day.
The hour spent willing myself out of bed
Was met with the crippling emptiness
Of reading emails of responsibility
And the burdening weight
Of a burnt-out student.
That hole in my chest
And clouds in my head
Lingered.
It was met with an overwhelming desire
To end it all.
Drop out,
Move on,
Make a massive change to maybe feel something.

I took my anti-depressants.
I hoped maybe,
Just maybe,
Things would look up.
I looked out and saw the blue sky,
And for a split second,
I was at peace.

And it's been a while since I've felt it.

"11:11 pm"

I feel like I'm floating on air.
This numbness has its clouds
Cushioning me as I drift along.
Quite honestly, it seems less and less likely
That I still have some semblance of control.
Rather, I must surrender,
And at least try to see
If there's another way out of this hole.

"11:17 pm"

Perhaps my biggest blunder
Was allowing myself to believe
What the world told me.

All of the times I spoke down on myself
And hid my greatness
Were ploys to destroy the spark of divinity
Within me.

And it's in you too.

I have hidden myself for too long,
And I want to grow as an individual,
But sometimes I feel like all I am doing
Is watching from the sidelines.
I am merely here.
And I'm not quite sure what to do from there.

"11:22 pm"

I tend to feel nothing
After feeling everything.
To stimulate and reap senses I crave to sense
Makes me feel immortal for mere minutes
Or hours or days,
But never lasting.

Rather, I end up in a pit
Of my own disregard for myself,
Digging deeper with every slit into my soul.

Focus in,
Focus here,
Focus on this angle for this shot
Because it will fade to black
Without a thought or control,
Merely thought-control of me.

I long to be emancipated from my mind,
From the control,
Yet I am exhausted from feeling too little;
I am willing to accept
What I at all other times would not,
And that is silence.
The silence is too loud at other times,
And I struggle to hear my own thoughts,
If they wish to be heard at all.

Perhaps it'd be best
To break the deafening noise.
Perhaps it'd be best
To dive deeper and deeper and deeper
Into triplets of emotions and poetry.

There is no theory.
There are no metaphors.
There is only me
And the thoughts I should've said before.

TRYING TO REPLACE YOU

ISN'T WORKING

"11:27 pm"

How terrible a curse it is
That I want you to save me
From you.

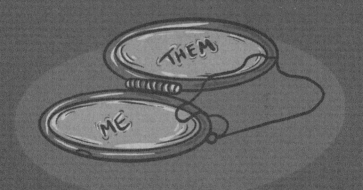

"11:33 pm"

Cigarette smoke never tasted so sweet,
And now it is my release.
The drugs I took for fun
Became the drugs I took to live,
And coffee-ringed paper became my only friend.
So, with coffee and cigarettes
Staining my teeth,
I clean the stains you left,
Working out the knots and licking my wounds.

My writing and mind become scattered;
I try to figure out my cypher
So that I can find some idea of understanding.
Yet, the letters and thoughts remain jumbled,
And I simply hope for the best.

Honestly though,
Holding on to hope
Is like holding on to the edge of a cliff,
And my fingers are starting to slip.

...ecoming a dream,
...oundtrack.

...n repeat.
...he new,
Discover the new.
Make the world as brilliant as your mind,
Brilliantly beautiful.
Should we ever stop creating
A new life
Of the dreaded and excited future?
Not dreaded for fear,
Dreaded because I don't know if I can keep up,
If I can make every miniscule moment matter.

"11:55 pm"

I create
To feel.
I feel
To create.
For some odd reason though,
Both tear my life apart.

I see it in you.
That inner artist is dying to come out,
Even though you yourself
Are struggling to hang on to dear life.

Please, never die.
Continue to live
Because the world needs you
And your art.

Your art is you.

I need you.

Please.

"11:59 pm"

These days I feel unused
And demised to self-judgement,
Destroying myself from the inside-out,
Crippling in anxiety.
My only moment of strength
Is my rare hope
Of released restraint.

Maybe after I will breathe free.
Maybe after I will feel again.
Maybe it will all be okay.

In reality,
I am living in yesterday,
Not today.
For today
I am strong.
I am my genius.
My self is conscious,
Pursuing today
And owning tomorrow.

"12:01 am"

The candle here
Flickers for me.
It ignites my senses
And calms the sea
Of uncertainty.

We are destroyed
And rebuilt,
Just like fire.
My guilt
Will remain in me to wilt.

I shall reexamine
What brought this discourse.
I remember the nights I was left alone
As my mind grew hoarse
Until all that was left was the remorse.

Thus, I yield.

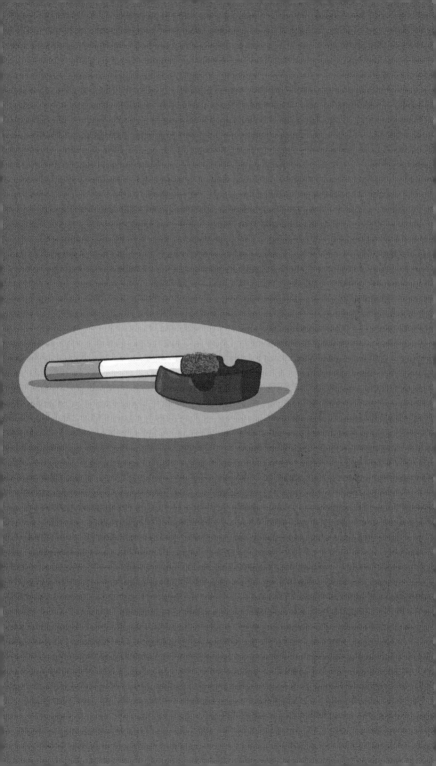

"12:09 am"

We create the analogies
And new worlds
And new stories
Through music and writing and art in our heads.
We create time and time again
To simply feel that which others feel.

I curiously discover it all,
The theories of our new lifestyle,
Our old lifestyle,
The collection of the collective.
We create and create and create
With love on our side.
So, I ask you, please,
Make me new,
Make me again,
Make me want to live.

"12:12 am"

You might only have one truth in your life.

Although I hope it doesn't happen,
One day you may have to choose
The one thing that matters most.
It may be tomorrow or next week or next year
Or never.
But if it comes down to it,
Trust yourself.

That one thing
May be the only thing
That's keeping you alive.

"12:15 am"

Why do I write?
I say the same shit over and over
Criticizing myself
And doing more harm than good.
I guess the possibilities are endless,
And hopefully I am too.

"12:18 am"

Can I say that I survived yet?
I've made it this far,
Over eight years of this bullshit,
And I have the scars to show for it.
Do I get to say that I lived?
I did after all,
Even if the pain still lingers.
Can I win when my enemy survives?
Sometimes that makes it hard for me to carry on,
Even though I've conquered it all
Every single time before.

When you enter a war,
You expect it to end at some point,
But this war has never ended, only subsided,
And then coming back with a vengeance.
I won't give up fighting,
I've come too far for that.
I guess I'll have to make due
With celebrating each battle won
And fighting on until victory.

It's life or death after all.

"12:22 am"

Letting go feels like the initial breath
After that first line.
The drip of release
Surges my mind
Deeper to a place I never want to leave.
I crave it more and more,
To purge myself
Of that which does not serve me.
I will be free,
But without it I am withdrawn.
So, I will dive back in
Until I reach the bottom of the sea,
Until I can finally reclaim me.

"12:28 am"

I am the dream I never dreamed,
And the answer to the question
I forgot to ask.
In my body lives the universe,
So truly it is not too big.
And thankfully, you're here too.

Collecting the tax on my life left me broken,
And now I rise from my own ashes.

These thoughts flow and spill out,
Creating the dots and dashes and Caesar shifts
That maybe someone can decipher.

The world spins, and I watch.
Time passes, and I am present.
I believe in myself
Because maybe,
Just maybe,
I can make it out alive this time.

"12:34 am"

I'm in infinite motion
Around my derelict mind,
Alone,
Lonely,
And lying to myself about both.

I'm surrounded constantly
By constant pounding,
And the constants become inconsistent
Until relativity becomes irrelevant.

I'm pulled over on the side of the road
Waiting for something,
Anything,
To make me believe that my impurity
Is purified.

Call me a water filter then,
And my multistep process
Becomes processed,
Factory made,
A copy
Of a copy
Of a copy
Of an original
Whom I no longer recognize.

Rebirth is not in the instruction manual,
And they don't teach sadness in high school.
I'm on my own in this one.

Well, I never am, honestly;
I do have you.

At the very least,
The spark is there.

"12:39 am"

The light in your eyes was a beacon,
Shining out of your illuminating, hopeful soul.
Like a ship lost at sea,
It guided me to safety
In you.

You didn't notice,
Well, you usually didn't,
That even in front of the most breathtaking views
All I could keep my eyes on
Was you.

The times I felt the most love for you
Were the moments when your eyes lit up
With a smile stretched as far as it could.
The pure joy that filled you
Caught me.

I think the reason this hurts so much
Was because I saw that fire dim.
The world stole your naivety,
And in turn,
It stole you.

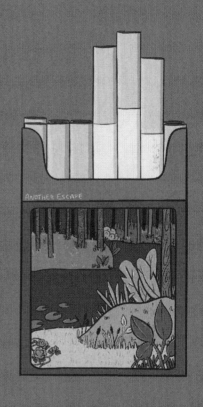

"12:43 am"

She often says
"You ground me, love."
But where is the ground,
And where am I?
Up in the air?
Without a care?
Without a need?

I stand here as I heed
That I am No Good Deed
Left Undecreed.
I simply wish to be a part of this,
Wishing it will be all right.
When will it be right?

"12:47 am"

I left the gaping hole in my chest open,
Hoping you would come by and fill me up.
All I needed
Was to realize the hole was not yours to fill.

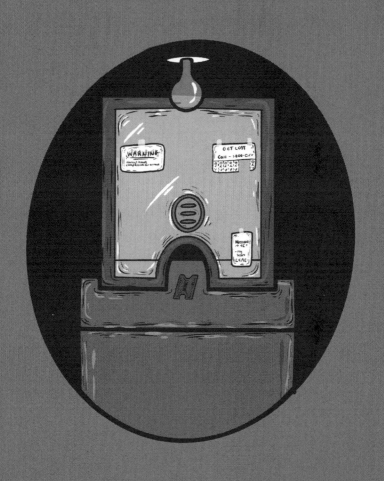

"12:52 am"

Do not free me
From the peripherals
Of my emotions.
I will continue to move
In directions of unknown destinations,
Seeing the smoke filling the car
Only to evaporate.

Eviscerate me of this motive
To burn my flesh;
Blow out the candle as it falls on me.

The cavity of my heart
Implodes
With every
Beat,
Until one day it bursts from me.

The doves fly away as I fall to my knees
With bloody knuckles
And a bloody temple;

I am my temple
And you are my deity.
I kneel in worship
After being beaten into submission.

Compare and contrast
The eventuality
Of exasperation,
Of encapsulation.
Where do I find this peace?

This inner mindset
Is a reset,
A removal
Of the inexplicable notion
That I am not alive.

"1:01 am"

"What ifs" are the things
That cause dreams to falter.

ld and explode
he life-force
at his own expense.

chine own
ngdom returns.
come the legacy
gst tidal waves and gods.

Dare not read your own self
Or you will find blank pages.

Pity or not,
You receive no scars
Of mine own accord,
Only of the record
Of my own life.

"1:11 am"

A natural disaster is beautiful.
It is not in the sense of the damage it causes,
Rather, it is because the damage can be directed
To a definite source,
Unlike my own damage
Which stems from everywhere.

I hear words of missing the old me,
However, I don't miss me.
I don't miss the mistakes
And the pain and regret.

I will not be myself again
Because after hurricanes we rebuild,
And I am being rebuilt
To become the new, true me:
The me I've always meant to be.

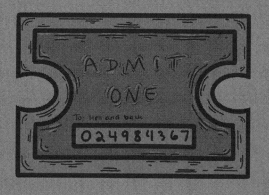

"1:19 am"

A touch
A glimpse
A simple expression of something
I find unexplainable

The difference is fallible
Between the thoughts I'm not sure
Are remorse or intrigue
Or somewhere in the middle

Her voice
Her lips
Her soul
I miss it

Should I regret that?

"1:26 am"

My emotions are hard as stone,
But I fret not,
For if nature can rewrite riverbanks,
I can rewrite the engravings that I fear.

If these words you do not believe,
Then ignore them.
One day, you will look back and see
That every letter means the world to you now.

"1:32 am"

You frequent my memories for some reason.
I'm not sure what we were, but, well, we were.
And that saved my life.

We decided one day,
Well, you did really,
That we'd be nudge buddies,
And that was that.
You picked me up
And nudged me along,
And along I came.

I learned slowly at first
What it was like to have friends.
Although shy,
I said hello,
And I spoke when spoken to.

You invited me out every so often,
To experience what would become the beginning
Of who I am today.

And even when the tide turned,
Even when I had to be the one to nudge you along,
We would still end up side by side.

Though distance persists,
We do too.

We conquered hell.
And we aren't afraid to use it.

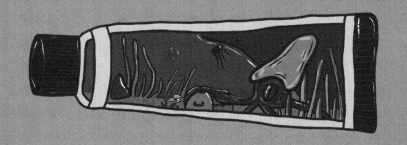

"1:38 am"

I want us to grab coffee,
Maybe sit down in the nearby park
And just talk for a while;
It's been years after all.

Maybe we can recount our memories
Of the streets and people around us,
Names that are now simply memories or tombstones.
We'll reminisce our childhoods
And the high school we hated that shaped us:
You, me, and all the other misfits
That seem to have found our niche.

We'll sip our coffees –
Lattes with white mocha,
Dark mocha and caramel –
And we'll remember all the ways we lived:
From the concerts in garages, barn attics,
Basements, and an old museum,
To that one house where we would smoke pot
And start to figure life out,
Even if we didn't fully get it at the time.

Things have changed, yes,
But the loaded emotions of our transition
From then
To now
Will always linger in this urban air.

"1:44 am"

There is no hope
As people settle for who they are
And become complacent to their current existence;
And yet there are those who dare otherwise:
The warriors.
They are those who fight every day,
Tooth and nail,
To own who they are.
They choose to stand up
And put on their war paint,
Resilient and refusing to go down
Without a fight.
They brawl every day
Against who the world thinks they should be.
And right now,
These warriors are winning.

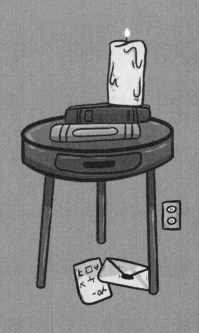

"1:49 am"

You came to me in a storm,
Ripping my every being apart,
Tearing up my roots to leave in the breeze.

How beautiful a storm you were,
And how lucky I am to rebuild from it.

WHEN WILL I REALISE

THAT I CAN BE FREE?

"1:56 am"

Why have we given up so much of the light
That we have found along the way?
Every breathtaking moment in history,
Every tremendous win for the light,
Was celebrated
And forgotten.

We lost so much of our hope
Because we keep holding on for something more,
While at the same time,
Not even realizing
That the "more" we keep seeking
Is right now.
In this moment.
And you can't keep hiding from it.

"2:05 am"

We were born into a world of black and white,
Seeking color to fulfill our grayscale souls
Every day, dripping splat after splat of color
Until we became an acid trip of moving hue.

Never once did we stop to think
Of how the paint on our canvas
Would bounce off us
And color those around us;
Whether our darkest colors
Would muddy the pastel,
Or our brightest hues
Would accent the dark canvases.

"2:09 am"

You need to know something:
I am building from the ground up.

I have been beaten and trampled and crushed,
A withering flower so desperate to feel the sun
again.

I am coming from the brink of self-destruction,
And truly, all I have is you.

You raised me up when I hit rock-bottom,
Lowering a ladder,
Helping me get out of this empty pit,
Offering a hand when no one else really would.

Honestly,
Who you are is subjective to the situation,
And no matter which situation it was,
You are important.

You saved me,
And like a beaten flower,
I will heal and grow and bloom.

So, thank you.

Whoever you are.

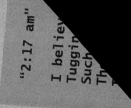

I believ
Tuggi
Such
Th

e your eyes are poetry
g at my heartstrings,
depth that I could fall forever.
problem that persists
s that I am accustomed to writing sad poetry,
And I cannot believe there is happiness
In my work,
Or in my life.
The concept is so foreign to me
That I don't even recognize it
Right in front of me
Staring back.

"2:22 am"

Do not make me your sunshine,
Or else I will burn you.
Make me your moonlight,
And I will illuminate your path in the night.

"2:25 am"

If people were nature,
You would be the sun
And I a flower,
For I cannot exist
Without your warmth
Or your light.

"2:29 am"

Cry me a river
Or cry me a song,
Yet hold back the tears for me.
Your eyes should glisten rarely,
Least of all
For someone who gave up
On his own accord.

Salinate your cheek with the sea,
Not the sea in your eyes.
I want to dive deep, deep into the deep blue,
A feeling of falling,
Falling,
Falling
Into inescapable you.

I am rich, my friend:
Rich in love with you.

Do you think there is one person for everyone?
Truly one person that is meant for your
Mind, Body, Heart, and Soul?

I.
"2:36 am"

I believe most heartbreak comes from finding a
person that only slightly fills us. There will
be that brilliant person who will rack your mind
senseless, and you will fall hopelessly in love
with their beautiful depth. However, that divide
will grow when they avoid your soft touch, too
afraid it will hurt them again as other hands have
in the past. You'll experience their thoughts as
nothing more in your life than the words in the
book that you never finished – it rests on your
nightstand while they lay next to you, and still a
million miles away.

Do you think there is one person for everyone?
Truly one person that is meant for your
Mind, Body, Heart, and Soul?

II.
"2:41 am"

After the heartache you'll discover who you think
may be divine incarnate, catching your eye the
very millisecond they enter the room. You'll
notice their smile first, somehow perfectly
genuine, somehow familiar, and somehow peaceful.
Their body is a perfect fit to yours, hands
snuggly together, or holding one another when it
seems like that might be your only chance at
happiness. But their eyes — their eyes will suck
you into their mountain range or ocean (or
wherever it lands in between) and then straight
into the black hole in the center. It will suck
you in, and then drift away. In the end, their
body was what you thought would love you, despite
their missing heart.

Do you think there is one person for everyone?
Truly one person that is meant for your
Mind, Body, Heart, and Soul?

III.
"2:43 am"

Soon after, a gentle hand will hold yours until
you see the light inside yourself again. They will
love you with all their heart until you can love
you with all of yours. It hits you – you may have
actually found The One. Still, as love comes so
too does it go, and you realize that all that love
is superficial. You honestly never find out why,
whether for status or financial or insanity, but
you fall under the impression that their supposed
love is as empty as their promises become. Maybe
they felt like they "saved you" - even though you
saved yourself - and they must search for their
next "project." You will move on, and you will
keep your worth with you.

Do you think there is one person for everyone?
Truly one person that is meant for your
Mind, Body, Heart, and Soul?

IV.
"2:51 am"

In the grand scheme of things, you may be one of
those people for someone else too. In time, we
learn and grow and learn to live on. Eventually
though, a wandering soul has learned the
lessons it's needed, finding you after you've
learned yours. It will feel like destiny the moment
you truly see each other. Your eyes will meet, and
they will understand. The past will come up
eventually and will rarely matter, and it will never
matter enough to push either of you away. The
longer you are together, the harder it will be
to separate your hearts and minds and bodies and
souls. There will be no resistance to love, as it
will pour between you fully and naturally and
beautifully overwhelming. They will love and cry
and trust and feel at every moment you do. And you
will do the same for them. And in that moment,
you'll realize that everything has finally fallen
into place.

"2:57 am"

I lost myself in the clouds,
Looking up, away, outward.
I felt myself slipping again,
Fading away
Into the space between the cotton candy skies.
I snapped back, feeling your fingers
Wrap between mine.
I looked at you, and I am here.
Thank you for always pulling me back.

"3:03 am"

I am on track for either my biggest win
Or lowest defeat,
And yet both are beautiful to me.
I stand at the crossroads of my life,
A place I know I will never stand again,
Yet the choice is no longer reluctant
Or shameful;
Instead, I stand here next to you
And look dead ahead,
Whatever direction ahead is.

I indite my autobiography as it plays out,
And for some reason
The chapters are getting smaller
And their impact more powerful than ever.

I pen a new chapter and title it Crossroads.

Each path beckons my name,
And I make the choice for myself;
No other person can play out the game
That I call my life
Better than I can.

I look down into the puddle in front of me,
Seeing my reflection.
The water is on fire,
The oceans of my eyes engulfed in flames,
Their desire to get on with life
Growing with unending intensity.

Maybe my dialect is drudging,
And I sound insane.
Or maybe, it's making sense for once
And I simply can't believe it.

I stand at the crossroads of my life
And I know which route is best.
I simply haven't figured it out yet.

"3:09 am"

There will come a day
When you wake up,
And you will know with absolute certainty
That you made it out alive.

The mortar fire in your head
Will have cease-fired,
And yet there will be no white flag
Raised by you.
The war may still rage,
But the battle will be won,
And your heart will make it home
In time for Christmas.

Trust yourself that this will happen.
You've made it this far.

"3:13 am"

Believe me when I say
That I am halfway up the mountain.
I have made it so far already,
That I am starting to forget
What that emptiness felt like,
Even if I still have such a long way to go.
The path hasn't been easy,
And I doubt it ever will be,
But I am so grateful to be on it.

I am full of wanderlust,
And what better journey than my life?

"3:21 am"

You know,
I never thought I would get this far.
A few years ago,
I could've sworn
That I would never see 20 years old.
That darkness consumed me,
Convincing me of no other possibility.

And here I am.

I made it this far,
So,
Fuck it.
I might as well see where this life is going.

"3:24 am"

As my spirit and mind blend,
I notice everything else slip away.
It feels almost impossible,
My own existence, I mean,
Since every second I feel like
I'm lost among the stars.

Where am I?
Everyone always asks me that,
And I remain without an answer
Because I'm not quite sure myself.

I guess this is the part
Where I start finding myself.

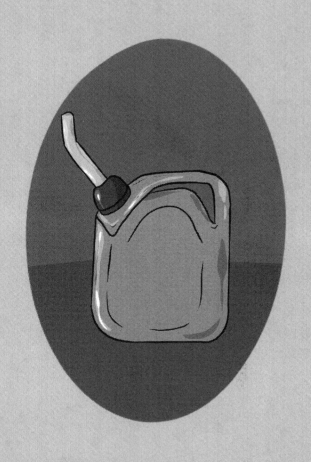

"3:33 am"

The key to life is gardening.
You constantly plant seeds of ideas,
Manifesting your reality.
You take nothing and turn it into everything.
However, like any seedling,
I can only grow,
If I am nurtured.
Nurture creates growth.
And all you need to do
Is remember to do the same
With yourself.

"3:37 am"

I saw one day a lavender
Tucked in a woman's hands.
I felt at peace and free,
And I smiled to myself.

Where the world went from there
No longer mattered
As joy took precedence,
Kindling my energy
Like a can of gasoline.

The patterns that appeared felt necessary,
And it all began to fall into place.

"3:43 am"

Oblivion is oblivion is oblivion,
And yet it is here with you.

There is beauty,
Unfathomable beauty,
Deep in your eyes.

I believe poetry exists
To describe you
And all you are.

And you are all to me.

I question myself,
Imagining my life without you,
Yet it is an imagination
I refuse to keep.

Believe me,
Please.

"3:49 am"

This time feels different.
For some odd reason,
I see myself next to you
With no end in sight.
The road we're following
Is that endless country road
That ends over the horizon,
And even that isn't definite.
And that's okay.

"3:54 am"

Where have I been all my life?
What legacy do I leave?

I live on in hearts and in pages of books,
And I live on in you.

As long as we keep each other afloat,
I guess that's all that really matters.

"4:00 am"

I rest upon a hilltop
Overlooking the vast meadows and forests
That capture my gaze.
I breathe in the fresh air,
Turning my head to the bright blue sky,
Watching the white clouds dance along
While I find what images hid within them.

I settled into the crisp green grass
And I felt the earth take hold of me.

"Memento Mori," I heard.

I smiled as I whispered in response,
"Dei Gratia."

"4:12 am"

If I had to
The moment
It'd be
I buil
And
No

choose
I knew it would turn out okay,
when you found the spark in me;
t the flame until it burned the sky
flickered with the stars.
t only did you hold up the mirror,
But through it I was able to truly see again.

"4:16 am"

If I'm being honest,
The days I wake up
And feel you next to me
Are the days I know everything will be okay.

"4:22 am"

Seldom do I forget to remember my existence.
I notice my own consciousness
And its capability to notice the patterns.

That's all life is really:
Patterns.
You notice them in the habits you form
And the music you hear and create.
The sun rises and falls,
The moon has its phases,
And you are awake or asleep.

Before you get too scared,
Thinking there is nothing but these patterns,
Simply remember
That if you play into the patterns,
You can create your own too.

"4:28 am"

There is a certain feel to aged wood.
You can almost feel the countless memories
As your fingertips brush over
The knots and splinters
Of the park bench it makes up.

Two names, or initials rather,
Carved into the birch
May remind you of when life seemed simpler
And more hopeful,
Despite the glistening fire still in you.

Maybe you'll look up and see them,
Running free and blissful
In a meadow of flowers.
As they do their delicate dance
Through the dandelions,
The fan will blow onto your heart's hearth.
You will remember
With ever-growing warmth and intensity
That it may truly turn out okay.

And you know you'll be okay too.

"4:32 am"

I feel free when I look up at the sky.
The infinite blue sucks me in,
Almost as easily as the blue in your eyes does.
I get lost in it,
And in that I find myself
Recognizing each moment
As new and beautiful.
That damned blue will get me every time,
Reminding me that I can truly find peace.

"4:40 am"

Where am I to stand
But in the Garden of Eden;
Your very presence is divine.
Your joy is infectious,
From a beautiful smile to illuminating eyes.

Keep that light in you lit.
The world needs it right now.

"4:44 am"

My heart doesn't normally know what it wants.
To be honest,
I'm quite content with almost anything.

There is, oddly, one exception,
One that I should've seen coming
Despite it flying deep out of left field:
You.

For some reason,
You caught me.
And I wouldn't want it any other way.

"4:51 am"

You are my fairytale,
And I know without a doubt
That it has a happy ending.
How do I know?
Well,
Let's just say
That I have a good feeling about this one.

"4:59 am"

Logically, your lips pressed to mine
Should not be as life-altering as it is.
And yet, even the slightest peck
Brings about the end of the world,
Only for it the begin again
The moment I open my eyes to see you.

"Hi," I whisper with a laugh.

"Hey," you reply with a smile that proves to me
That Eden is here with us.

"5:03 am"

Perhaps my greatest memory of us
Is the fact that we were an "us" to begin with.

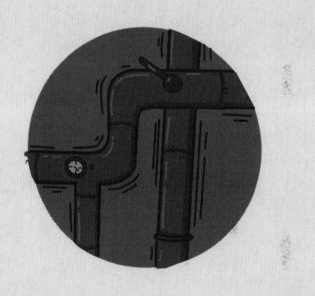

"5:09 am"

I don't ever want to dream again
Simply because I've seen you,
And that in itself
Is a dream come true.

"5:17 am"

It's 5:17 A.M.,
And I can't stop thinking
About how beautiful you are
And how easily
I can lose myself to you.

"5:25 am"

I guess we never tire of watching sunsets.
It's kind of like how I never tire
Of seeing you.

You, and all your radiant beauty.

"5:29 am"

I've never had a favorite color
Until the day I fell into the sea
Of your eyes.

"5:32 am"

I find love in your smile and eyes
And every little word
That I feel whispered in the air.
The words that I thought were lost to me
Land like tulip petals on my soul.
The juxtaposition of words
Feels lighter than air,
Snatching the breath straight from my lungs.
The irony when you say "I hate you"
As you blush after I express how I truly feel
Makes me want you to "hate me" even more.

"5:38 am"

Oh, the music I hear
That often reminds me of you
Makes me blissfully unaware
Of the surroundings I ignore.

I crave the freedom of the melody,
The experience of feeling at home,
The feeling that never leaves
When my mind settles on you.

Simplistic words
Strung together;
I will never forget them
As they traced us to one another.

They are intertwined
So long as the song plays in our hearts,
And the beat will not cease
Any time soon.

"5:41 am"

I want to kiss you under sunsets,
Listen to acoustic songs
From our favorite bands no one has ever heard of,
Laying helplessly in love
With each other and the life around us.

My fingertips brush against yours
So lightly as a feather,
Weathering away the walls
That for too long
Have held our hearts hostage.

I want to run.
Run with me,
Away from it all,
And run until my sunset kisses
Turn into moonlit love.

"5:47 am"

I often keep my work gender neutral,
Removing most identification
To allow space for your mind to make up
Whom the poem is about.

This is not one of those poems
Because as I stare into your eyes,
I see a nebula of color
That you pass off every day as ordinary,
Even though I can dive deeper and deeper
Into the galaxies you form.

Those beautiful chocolate eyes,
So evident of your sweetness,
Will catch me like a mouse trap every time.

Your eyes have this warmth
That I can only describe
As cuddling up under blankets
With hot cocoa in hand
After playing outside in the snow
For longer than we knew should,
Simply because we didn't want the moment to end.

And I don't want this moment to end either:
You, me, and our eyes lost in each other's depth.

"5:51 am"

I feel our arms intertwine
As you huddle close to me
In the brisk late-autumn air.
I catch your smile out of the corner of my eye,
And it can't help but be contagious.

We walk through the bustle of the city,
And we watch as the world slips by around us.
We walk through Central Park,
And we stop at every shop there is,
Simply because you asked.

We breathe in the fact
That the world has been yielded to us.
It's as if I'm taking a photograph:
You're my focus, and the rest is a blur.

I see your eyes light up at it all,
The falling leaves, the playful pups,
And the laughing people.

You love the little things,
And I love that.

And I love you.

"5:55 am"

I'm not too sure
When I stopped writing love poems.
The comparisons to stars and flowers
Fell to the ground with the autumn leaves.

Quite similarly, I fell into you.
I think that might've been when the pen strokes
Ceased.

Everything I had ever written,
Every butterfly in me,
Found a home in you.
And I did too.

"6:00 am"

My favorite moments with you
Are the subtle ones:
The shared moments
Of just us,
Tapping each other's feet under the table
Or giving light head scratches,
Or any of the small yet enormous gestures
That say, "I love you."

"6:03 am"

I got lost in the silence,
Your breath the only thing I heard –
The only thing I needed to hear.
Your warm breath kissed my skin
As I moved a small bit of hair behind your ear.
We cradled each other's faces,
And the world around us stopped.

I see you.
And you see me.
And sometimes,
That's all it takes to remind me
That happy endings can come true.

"6:09 am"

I want to fall into the constellations
Of your freckles and your eyes.
I want to kiss every inch of you,
And look you dead in the eye
And tell you "I love you"
Until you believe it as much as I do.

"6:14 am"

I will fall in love with you
Because I love your eyes.
I love the way they dart around,
Examining me and still full of love,
Exploring and feeling with no touch.
I love the way your eyes light up
When you enter that giddy state
That I know and love so well.

I will fall in love with you
Because I love your excitement.
I love kissing you while you radiate love,
And I love seeing you get excited
Over the little things.
I love your excitement over art and music
And the wonders of the world,
And I love that you are one of those wonders
To me.

I will fall in love with you
Because I love your passion.
I love how committed you are
To everything you set your mind to.
I love that you know your ambition
Like the back of your hand,
And I love that you want to push me
To reach mine.

I will fall in love with you
Because I love how loving you are.
I love the way you protect your own.
I love the way you actually care about people.
I love the way our hands fit perfectly together
And our heartbeats sync
When we lay side-by-side.

I will fall in love with you
Because I love your body.
I love the way you curl up into a ball
Right before you go to bed,
And I love the way you hug me tight.
I love the way you calm me
When the world seems to crash down around me.
I love the way your nose crinkles when you laugh,
And your smile captures my mind
Every second I get the chance to glimpse it.

I will fall in love with you
Because I love how much you love me.
I love the fact
That even though I hate being tickled,
You keep doing it
Simply to hear my laugh which you love so dearly.
I love that you'd drop everything
To be there for me,
And I love that you know
I would do the same for you.

I will fall in love with you
No matter how many times you warn me not to.
I will fall in love with you,
And there won't be a moment I regret it.

"6:16 am"

Expanding personal understanding
Can be exhausting.
You dig back up
Everything you wanted to remain buried,
And release it from your life.
You begin to tear down the walls
That for so long
You thought were there to protect you,
When really,
All they did was keep in all of the hurt.

Letting go
Of everything you once found familiar
That no longer serves you
Will be like climbing a mountain.
In the end though,
The view will be oh so worth it.

One day you'll feel free.
You'll wake up, breathe a new breath,
See the cloudy or clear skies,
And it will all
Be
Okay.

And that day is today,
Tomorrow,
And the day after times infinity.

"6:20 am"

I'm not quite sure who I started writing for,
And I am okay not knowing.
I write for myself now.
I write for the moments of fresh air,
The sunrises,
And the blue jays.
I write for the first day of freshman year
And for when it's time to walk across the stage
At graduation.
I write for a lot of things,
Yet none compare to you.

I often find myself living repetitions,
Hence some of my poems' repetitive nature.
The reason I do this
Is because I want to drive home a few points:
There is light, there is love,
And YOU. ARE. WORTHY.
Sometimes,
All we need is to be reminded those things;

So, that's what I'm here for.
You still have that spark,
And I am a billow,
Reminding you of what it feels like
To almost burn out,
And what it feels like
To burn to so bright
That the sun somehow becomes envious.
I'm here to remind you
That even though life can get dark,
You woke up today,
And that means your spark,
Or purpose if you want to call it that,
Is not burned out yet.

The poet Tyler Knott Gregson once wrote that
"There will always be light,
And I will never stop chasing it."

And that's all I have to say about that.

"6:29 am"

In the end, we will come full circle;
My reaching hand
Will grasp the stars
And I will move past the vestige of the darkness.

I will return to stardust,
And you will too.

And frankly,
I couldn't be happier
That our stardust found each other
Before conceding to the rising sun.

Acknowledgements

I would like to acknowledge the following people:

My abuelita and grandma, for raising me to become the man I am today, and for teaching me unconditional love.

My parents, for supporting me through thick and thin, and for teaching me that I can always pursue my dreams.

Adam, for being the best brother anyone could ask for, for guiding me through this hectic world, and for being an inspiration to me every day.

Nicole, for pushing me to see my true potential, for always having my back, and for being the best soul sister a guy could ask for.

Lily and Connor, for being some of my closest friends, and for the countless memories that have made you family.

Chris, for being an amazing editor, brother, and friend, and for always being authentic and fun.

Melissa, for always being a stand for me, for believing in me non-stop, and for being magical. Buddies for life.

My team, ML34 FLL, for being a continuous stand for me and my work, for teaching me invaluable lessons, and for becoming like family to me.

Jay, for continuously supporting me, and for being someone I can always look up to.
Best. Buddy. Ever.

Acknowledgements

I would also like to acknowledge:

Missy, LJ, Carolyn, for loving me and holding me high, even when I felt too low to get back up.

Dana, Todd, Wolfie, for somehow knowing exactly the right thing to say at the right time, and for believing in my greatness so much that I was finally able to see it too.

Sal, for never losing sight of yourself, for creating beautiful art, for being a brother, and for inspiring me to continue my work after our debut.

Shannon, for being there for me since the beginning, for being a total badass, and for never letting distance get between us.

Everyone, for seeing the light in me even when I was in darkness, for reminding me of how much I've grown, and for spreading light with me.

An extra special thank you to Rhea, for believing in this project since the beginning, for being an utterly wonderful human being, for your endless love to this world, for being one of my closest friends, and for creating magic and pouring your heart into this book.

Made in the USA
Lexington, KY
20 November 2019

57248857R00131